One-Minute
Greek Myths

Other books by the author:
One-Minute Bedtime Stories
One-Minute Favorite Fairy Tales
One-Minute Animal Stories
One-Minute Bible Stories—Old Testament
One-Minute Bible Stories—New Testament
with Florence Henderson

One-Minute Greek Myths

by

Shari Lewis

Research by Gerry Matthews

Illustrated by C. S. Ewing

DOUBLEDAY & COMPANY, INC.
GARDEN CITY, NEW YORK

To Gerry Matthews, my longtime friend, who
helped me see through these odd stories of the
gods of old, and behold myself.

Library of Congress Cataloging-in-Publication Data

Lewis, Shari.
   One-minute Greek myths.

   Summary: Retells twenty famous myths in a one-minute
format. Includes "Pandora's Box," "The Midas Touch,"
and "Hercules."
   1. Mythology, Greek—Juvenile literature.
[1. Mythology, Greek]   I. Matthews, Gerry.   II. Ewing,
C. S., ill.   III. Title.
BL782.L49   1987   292'.13   86–19683
ISBN 0-385-23423-6
ISBN 0-385-23849-5 (lib. bdg.)

CONTENTS

To the Parents

My relationship to Greek mythology is simply and delightedly on the level of "the story." I am trained neither as anthropologist, psychologist, or even as a thinker of any great depth. I am a performer and storyteller, grateful to do both to the best of my abilities and to the end of my days.

However, bringing stories of various cultures to life for young people has always seemed meaningful to me, and *these* bizarre legends of fantastic characters, flamboyant behavior, and exaggerated emotions will surely stimulate your child's imagination and sense of wonder.

As you introduce your kids to these One-Minute adventures, please don't let them know that they're getting "classical" Greek mythology. After all, if you play lively classical music around your house, your kids will enjoy it as the toe-tapping, finger-snapping delight that it is, *unless* you announce that classical music is "serious" stuff. Just present these stories as the weird and wonderful tales that they are, and your youngsters won't feel burdened to "learn" from them.

Of course, there *are* lessons here, hidden in each tale. King Midas's greed caused him to lose his beloved daughter. If Narcissus hadn't been so vain, he wouldn't have been transformed into a flower. Arachne's boastfulness got *her* turned into a spider. There are lessons here!

But Jean Houston, author of *Sacred Psychology*, says the lessons in myths are not always on the surface. She suggests that we can learn even from the mean actions and petty jealousies of the gods. Since they're like us in our negative behavior, perhaps we can be like them in their higher, finer ways. Recognizing the petty person in the gods, can we see our *own* potential for godliness? For benevolence? For grand achievements? For confidence? Reading about Theseus (who sailed for Crete with the children doomed to be fed to the monster), can we absorb the value of setting out bravely, without procrastination, to accomplish what we know *needs* to be done, even if we're not quite sure *how* we're going to do it?

For so-called grownups like me, the additional fun in reading these myths is in finally discovering the full meaning of oft-heard, little-understood clichés (like "cleaning out the Augean Stables," "Oedipus Complex," "Pandora's box," and so on).

It's extra nice when parents and children are exposed to quality material together—the youngsters just plain relish the stories while the adults can secretly enjoy the pleasure of "brushing up."

As the Greek gods are most commonly known by their Roman names, the latter are used here. What follows is both a list of Greek/Roman equivalents and a pronunciation guide to characters mentioned in this book.

Shari Lewis

Names

Greek name	Roman name	Greek name	Roman name
Aphrodite	Venus	Hephaestus	Vulcan
Ares	Mars	Hera	Juno
Athena	Minerva	Heracles	Hercules
Cronus	Saturn	Hermes	Mercury
Demeter	Ceres	Mnemosyne	Memoria
Dionysus	Bacchus	Ops	Rhea
Eros	Cupid	Persephone	Proserpina
Hades	Pluto	Zeus	Jupiter

Pronunciations

Accented syllable is underlined and capitalized

Andromeda	An-<u>DRAW</u>-mĕ-duh	Oedipus	<u>ĔD</u>-ĭ-puss
Arachne	Ă-<u>RACK</u>-nee	Omphale	<u>UM</u>-fuh-lee
Centaur	<u>SEN</u>-tōr	Pandora	Pan-<u>DOOR</u>-uh
Ceres	<u>SEE</u>-reez	Parnassus	Par-<u>NASS</u>-us
Daedalus	<u>DED</u>-uh-lus	Perseus	<u>PER</u>-see-us
Dejanira	Day-uh-<u>NEE</u>-ruh	Phineus	<u>FINE</u>-ee-us
Deucalion	Du-<u>KAL</u>-yen	Prometheus	Pro-<u>MEE</u>-thee-us
Epimetheus	Ep-ĭ-<u>MEE</u>-thee-us	Proserpina	Pro-ser-<u>PEE</u>-na
Icarus	<u>Ĭ</u>-kuh-rus	Pyrrha	<u>PEE</u>-ruh
Iphitus	<u>IF</u>-uh-tus	Rhea	<u>REE</u>-uh
King Minos	<u>MY</u>-nōs	Salinus	Suh-<u>LINE</u>-us
Marsyas	<u>MAR</u>-see-us	Thebes	Thēbz
Medusa	Mĕ-<u>DOO</u>-suh	Theseus	<u>THEE</u>-see-us
Muses	<u>MIU</u>-sez	Titans	<u>TEI</u>-tanz
Narcissus	Nar-<u>SĬSS</u>-uhs		

How It All Began

According to the ancient Greeks, who lived a long, long time ago, it all began in darkness. Land, water, and air were mixed in a whirling mess called Chaos. Land was almost liquid, water was almost solid, and air was a little of both. Nature straightened it all out and made Earth look as it does today.

Then came a race of giant gods called Titans, who were taller than mountains. A Titan named Prometheus was chosen to create man. He took dirt and water and made a man that looked like himself, only much smaller. And, unlike the four-legged animals that went around staring at the ground all the time, Prometheus made man stand up straight, so he could see the stars. But without sharp claws or teeth (like the lion) to use

8

as weapons or long legs (like the giraffe) with which to run, this man couldn't protect himself. And without a fur coat (like the bear's) he couldn't keep warm in the winter. So Prometheus lit a torch from the chariot of the sun, brought the fire down from heaven, and gave it to man.

With fire, man was able to forge metal to make weapons for his protection and tools to help him grow food. And in winter, when snows piled up, he could huddle near the fire and keep warm and snug until spring.

9

Mount Olympus

The king of the giant Titans, Saturn, had become king by chasing off his own father. Afraid *his* children would do the same to him, every time his wife, Rhea, had a baby, Saturn would swallow it, to make sure his throne was safe. Rhea grew tired of having her babies swallowed, so when little Jupiter was born, she hid him, and dressed a stone in baby clothes. Saturn (who apparently could eat anything), swallowed the stone without knowing the difference.

His mother sent Jupiter off to the country to be brought up by a goat. When he was big and strong, Jupiter forced his father Saturn to vomit his brothers and sisters (who had been living in Saturn's stomach all those years). Together they chased the old king away.

Jupiter became king of the gods and made twelve of his brothers, sisters, and children into gods and goddesses, too. They moved from earth up to behind the clouds at the top of Mount Olympus. In beautiful brass palaces, Jupiter and his

queen Juno sat with the others on golden thrones, drank nectar, and ate ambrosia (both of which were delicious enough to be considered food for the gods). Apollo (god of music and poetry) played music on his lyre, the Muses (the nine goddesses in charge of entertainment) sang wonderful songs. In golden shoes, they all went for walks on the water and through the air. They rode magic chariots across the heavens. On top of all that, they were immortal, which means they could live forever. No question about it, it was good to be a god.

Pandora's Box

Jupiter was angry at Prometheus for stealing fire from the sun and giving it to humans. To get even with Prometheus, Jupiter told the gods and goddesses on Mount Olympus to create a gorgeous woman for him to send down to earth.

Jupiter named the woman Pandora and gave her a box. "If you know what's good for you," he said, "you'll never, ever open this box." Pandora agreed and was sent down to earth as a gift to Prometheus.

Prometheus, who didn't trust Jupiter, wouldn't let Pandora in the door. But his brother, Epimetheus, begged Pandora to become his wife, and she moved right in.

For a while, Pandora enjoyed herself. But one day she got bored and decided to take just a tiny peek inside the box Jupiter had given her. She pried open the lid. Out flew the devils and

demons Jupiter had hidden in the box. They swarmed over the earth, making everyone sick and miserable. Pandora felt awful, but one important thing had *not* escaped from Pandora's box, and that was hope. When Pandora saw hope still in there, it is said that she felt better, for hope is the one thing without which we cannot exist!

The Flood

The first people on earth were happy folks without many problems. Because the weather was always nice, they slept under the stars. Fruit hung from every tree, so there was plenty to eat. Everyone got along fine.

But as time passed, things changed. Winters grew cold, and people had to build shelters in which to live. Fruit was no longer there for the picking, so people were forced to grow food. As life became harder, neighbors argued, wars broke out, robbers roamed the countryside, and love and friendship disappeared from the face of the earth.

Angry, Jupiter said to the gods, "I've decided to start

over." He caused rains to flood the earth and everyone drowned except for Deucalion and his wife Pyrrha, the only man and woman who hadn't been bad. They were stranded on top of Mount Parnassus with waves lapping at their sandals when Jupiter ordered an end to the flooding. "You will start a new race of people," he told the frightened couple. "Pick up stones and throw them over your shoulders." Deucalion and Pyrrha did, and each stone turned into a new person as it hit the ground. His stones became men, hers became women. And that is supposed to be how mankind got off to a rocky new start.

15

Apollo

Apollo, the god of music and poetry, was known to be a sore loser.

There was the time Apollo heard about a satyr named Marsyas who was supposed to be as good a musician as he.

Now, satyrs weren't powerful gods like the ones on Mount Olympus. They were little half-men/half-goat characters who danced in the woods and played their flutes. Nevertheless, Apollo challenged Marsyas to a contest.

When Marsyas heard Apollo strum his golden lyre (which was like a harp), his mouth went dry because Apollo was so good. But when it was Marsyas's turn, he played his flute so well, the Muses (those goddesses of entertainment, who really knew their stuff), couldn't decide who was better.

16

Apollo, really angry, said he'd try again—only this time, they would play their instruments *upside down* and sing at the same time!

Now, Apollo had no trouble strumming his lyre upside down, because you can pluck the strings either way, and since you strum with your fingers, singing at the same time presents no problem. But poor Marsyas was unable to fit his fingers to the holes of the upside down flute, and he could hardly sing and blow into the flute at the same time, could he? And so our friend Apollo won the contest.

The Midas Touch

King Midas, who loved gold, was forever fondling his golden rings and things, and running his fingers through his coin collection. Midas loved his daughter, too, but he spent more time with his golden trinkets than with her.

One day, a satyr named Salinus, (who was half man, half goat), asked if he could spend the night. Midas knew that Salinus was a good friend of Bacchus, the god of wine, so he invited the old goat in. "Always keep on the good side of the gods," Midas thought, and he gave a party that went on for a week.

Afterward, the satyr told the god Bacchus that King Midas had treated him well. Pleased, Bacchus insisted that Midas pick his own reward. "Fix it so that everything I touch turns to gold," said Midas. Bacchus frowned but granted the wish, and sure enough, everything Midas touched turned to gold: first, his chair, then his dinner, and, when he hugged her, even his beloved daughter.

Midas was miserable, alone in a golden palace full of golden people and hard gold food that he couldn't eat.

He prayed to Bacchus to undo the wish (which had turned into a curse). Bacchus did. Midas's food no longer turned to gold when it touched his lips, but before he ate a bite, it is said that Midas gave his daughter a big hug.

Proserpina

Pluto was god of the underworld, where people went after they stopped living. It wasn't a cheerful place, and Pluto wanted a wife to liven things up down there. He went to see Jupiter, who said, "Ceres, the goddess of all the fruits of the earth, has a daughter named Proserpina. You can marry her, *if* you can get her to go with you."

Pluto flew off and found Proserpina picking daffodils. He didn't bother asking. He just grabbed her and down they went to his place.

Ceres heard what happened to her daughter, and went to Mount Olympus to have it out with Jupiter. "Let my daughter come home," she threatened, "or I'll fix it so nothing will grow on the face of the earth and everyone will starve."

20

Jupiter knew she had him. "All right, she can come back," he declared, "*if* she hasn't eaten anything while in the underworld."

When Pluto heard that he had to give up his bride, he questioned the servants. One of them said he'd only seen Proserpina chewing on a few pomegranate seeds.

After a lot of arguments on Mount Olympus, it was decided that Proserpina could stay with her mother for nine months of the year but would have to return to the underworld the other three. And every year since then, while Proserpina is underground with Pluto, Ceres has made the earth turn cold, and nothing will grow for those three wintry months.

Echo

A nymph named Echo loved to talk, but she always *had* to have the last word.

One day, in a woodland pool, Jupiter was playing games with the water nymphs. Echo spotted Jupiter's wife, Juno, looking for him. She knew that if Juno caught Jupiter with the nymphs, Juno would be jealous, so Echo blocked the goddess's path and started talking. "Why, Juno," said Echo, "what a lovely robe you've got on. Where in heaven did you get it?" She prattled on and on, saying nothing but keeping Juno busy.

Meanwhile, back at the pool, the water nymphs heard

Echo's words, realized what was going on, and swam away fast to avoid Juno's jealous temper.

Later, when Juno found out what Echo had done, she cast a spell on the talkative little nymph, fixing it so Echo could only *repeat* what was said to her. Echo would still have the last word, but she could no longer speak first. This made Echo very unhappy. Unable to chatter, she wandered off into the hills and wasted away to nothing. But her voice remains even to this day, and if you are in the hills, Echo will probably repeat *your* last words for you, too.

Narcissus

Narcissus was a handsome young man with blond curls and rippling muscles, but he was mean to girls. Whenever a nymph or a sprite fell in love with him, he made fun of her or acted as though she didn't exist.

One little nymph prayed that some day, *Narcissus* would feel the pain of being ignored by someone *he* loved. The nymph's prayer was heard on Mount Olympus and the gods laid a trap for Narcissus.

Next day, when Narcissus leaned down to drink at a pond, he saw his own reflection mirrored on the surface and instantly fell in love with *himself.* He tried to kiss his own beautiful face

24

before him, but when his lips touched the water, the reflection disappeared among the ripples. Each time his face reappeared, Narcissus tried to touch it, and each time, it went away. For weeks, the conceited fellow did nothing but reach for himself in the water.

After a while, having forgotten to eat he starved to death. The nymphs went to bury Narcissus, but there was no trace of his body. Instead, where he had been, there now grew a beautiful yellow flower, its head leaning toward the pond, admiring its reflection. That flower has been called Narcissus ever since.

Arachne

Minerva, goddess of spinning and weaving, was considered the best with needle and thread. But a time came when a young girl on earth named Arachne was thought to be almost as good. Even nymphs came out of the woods to see the beautiful tapestries Arachne made. Unfortunately, Arachne began boasting that she could beat the goddess in a weaving contest any time.

Minerva disguised herself as an old woman and visited Arachne. "If you keep bragging," she said, "Minerva's liable to get mad." Arachne replied, "If that goddess thinks she's better than me, let her prove it."

With that, Minerva dropped her disguise. Arachne wasn't worried. She began to weave a tapestry unlike anything that had been seen before.

26

Furious at this lack of respect, the goddess Minerva bopped Arachne on the head and changed the proud girl into a humble servant.

Realizing how rude she'd been to the goddess, Arachne tried to hang herself with some of her yarn, but Minerva didn't want her to die. She waved her hand and turned Arachne into a spider hanging in her web.

And Arachnida is what the class of spiders is known as, from that day to this!

Medusa and Perseus

Medusa was a hideous monster with hissing snakes on her head, long sharp fangs and claws of brass. Medusa was so ugly, no living thing could look at her without turning to stone. The cave where she lived was surrounded by stony statues of people and animals that had accidentally caught sight of her and were petrified on the spot. Once in a while, Medusa went out and turned whole villages of people into piles of rocks. Finally, it got so bad that Perseus was sent to see what he could do about the problem.

Though he wasn't a god himself, Perseus, son of the god Jupiter, had friends on Mount Olympus. They loaned him a shiny shield and a pair of winged shoes that enabled him to fly.

Using those winged shoes, Perseus approached Medusa's cave without making a sound. He stepped inside and there was Medusa. She was asleep but the snakes on her head were awake and they threatened Perseus. To avoid looking at her directly and being turned into stone, Perseus only watched her *reflection*, mirrored in the shiny surface of his shield. As the snakes writhed and hissed, Perseus lifted his sword and cut off Medusa's ugly head.

29

Atlas and Perseus

Perseus cut off Medusa's head, put it in his pack, and flew on his winged shoes until he came to the end of the earth.

This was the country of King Atlas, the biggest and nastiest man around. When he saw Perseus, Atlas said, "Hey you! What do you want?" Perseus introduced himself as Jupiter's son, and told Atlas that he'd just killed Medusa. "I'd appreciate a sandwich and maybe a glass of milk, and I'll be on my way," said Perseus with a winning smile.

"I don't care who your father is," shouted Atlas, lunging at Perseus with his massive sword.

But Perseus was a tricky fighter. He sidestepped the giant and pulled out Medusa's head, which, as you may remember, he was carrying in

his sack. Keeping his own eyes closed, he held up the ugly head for Atlas to see, and the big king turned to stone. But Atlas was *so* enormous that he became a mountain, with trees growing out of his beard and snow on the top of his head. And for some reason, he continued to grow in size until his shoulders reached the starry sky. And according to Greek mythology, Atlas is there to this day, holding the heavens in place.

Perseus and Andromeda

After cutting off Medusa's head, Perseus flew along the coast. He passed a girl named Andromeda, who was chained to a rock. "What happened to you?" he asked.

"Oh, it's my mother's fault," cried the maiden. "She made the gods angry, and they sent a sea-monster to attack our country. The monster has said that the only way to make peace is for me to be his next meal. Monsters prefer maidens to mothers, it seems." At that moment, the monster surfaced in the ocean and headed straight for them.

"Tell you what," said Perseus. "If I can kill this thing, you and I will be married." On his winged shoes, Perseus flew to the monster and

plunged his sword into its back. The beast curled up in agony, belched a lot of black smoke, and died.

During the wedding party for Perseus and Andromeda, a fellow named Phineus arrived with his troops. "Andromeda is supposed to marry me!" shouted Phineus, and his soldiers attacked Perseus and the wedding guests. Perseus pulled Medusa's head out of his sack and held it high. "All my friends close their eyes," shouted Perseus. "The rest of you, look what I've got!" Of course, Phineus and his soldiers looked at the head of Medusa and turned to stone, and the two young lovers were able to get on with their wedding.

Jason and the Golden Fleece

Jason knew that he had to steal a golden sheepskin from a vicious dragon before his evil uncle would let him become the next king. With fifty men, Jason crossed the ocean in a boat called the Argo.

A sorceress (a lady magician) named Medea gave Jason a magic charm to keep him safe.

When they reached the other shore, *before* Jason could steal the sheepskin from the dragon, he had to plant some teeth from *another* dragon (one that had already been killed in *another* story).

Jason planted the dragon's teeth. Instantly, an army of angry soldiers grew up out of the earth, like corn. They attacked Jason, but he threw the sorceress's magic charm among them, and they killed each other instead.

Now Jason approached the vicious dragon guarding the fleecy golden sheepskin. No one had ever gotten past this dragon, because it absolutely *never* slept. But Medea gave Jason a magic powder which, when sprinkled in front of the dragon, caused it to close its eyes and go off to dreamland. Jason quickly snatched that golden sheepskin, dashed to his boat Argo, and returned home to claim his throne. And realizing how valuable a sorceress can be in a tight spot, Jason not only took Medea home with him, but he married her, as well!

Oedipus

The king of Thebes, afraid that his baby son would grow up and murder him, ordered a passing traveler to get rid of the little boy. The traveler hung the infant on a tree by one foot and left him there to die, but a peasant rescued the baby, and named him Oedipus, which means Bigfoot.

    Years later, the king's chariot was blocked on a narrow road by a young man coming toward him. They argued, and the king was killed by the young man who, by a strange coincidence, was Oedipus, his own son.

Down the road, Oedipus was challenged by the Sphinx, a monster with the body of a lion and the head of a woman. "Answer my riddle or die," snarled the Sphinx. "What animal walks on all fours in the morning, on two feet at noon, and on three in the evening?" "Easy," Oedipus replied, "the animal you describe is man. Early in life, as a baby, he crawls. In the middle of his life, he stands on his own two feet. And in old age, he adds a cane."

The Sphinx dropped dead on the spot, and the people of Thebes made Oedipus their king. They even gave him the old king's wife, Queen Jocasta, as his bride. But Jocasta was really his mother, and when she found out she had married her own son, she killed herself.

Then Oedipus went mad and poked out his own eyes. As you can see, Greek myths don't all have happy endings!

Theseus and the Minotaur

On the Isle of Crete, there was a monster called a Minotaur, which was half-man and half-bull. It lived in a labyrinth (a puzzling area with many crossing and twisting paths from which it was hard to escape). This monster belonged to King Minos of the Isle of Crete, who supplied his monster with young people to eat. Every year, seven boys and seven girls were sent from the city of Athens to be devoured by the horrible Minotaur.

When Theseus heard about this, he decided to go along and kill the Minotaur, or die trying. His father, the king of Athens, tried to talk him out of it, but Theseus wouldn't listen.

The boat left for Crete with a black sail on it to let everyone know that those on board would not be coming back. "If I'm successful," Theseus told his father, "I'll return under white sail instead of black." At Crete, the boys and girls were taken to see King Minos before being sent off to the Minotaur. Minos's daughter Ariadne was there, and she fell in love with Theseus. As he was led away, certainly to die, she slipped him a magic sword and a spool of thread. With this sword, Theseus killed the monster, and, following the trail of thread he had strung behind him, led the boys and girls out of the labyrinth. They returned to Athens, but in their excitement, forgot to raise the white sail. When Theseus's father saw the boat enter the harbor under a black sail, he died of grief, and that's how Theseus became king of Athens.

Daedalus and Icarus

Daedalus built things for kings. For Minos, king of Crete, he built the labyrinth with its puzzling paths, in which Minos kept his monster, the Minotaur. But later, Minos decided he didn't like Daedalus and locked him in a tower with his son, Icarus. To escape, Daedalus built two pairs of wings made of feathers left

by sea birds nesting in the tower. He sewed some of the feathers, others he glued in place with wax.

He taught his son, Icarus, to fly, and they were ready to escape from the island. Daedalus said, "Son, don't get close to the waves or your wet wings will be heavy and you won't be strong enough to flap them. And stay far from the sun, for the heat will surely melt the wax and the feathers will come loose."

Then, father and son flapped their wings and flew away from their tower prison and off across the ocean to freedom. But, excited by the fun of flying, Icarus forgot what his father had said. He chased a sea gull high above the clouds. As he got closer to the sun, its heat melted the wax from his wings, the feathers fell off, and Icarus tumbled into the sea and drowned.

Hercules

When Hercules was only a few minutes old, someone dropped two nasty snakes into his crib in order to kill him. But baby Hercules strangled them—and that was just the beginning of his strength!

Later, he killed a lion that had been bothering farmers. He wrestled that lion to the ground and strangled it to death. Then, he pulled off its skin and wore it as a cloak, with the lion's head as a helmet. The king, pleased to get rid of the lion, offered Hercules his fifty daughters as a token of gratitude. But Hercules wasn't ready to settle down and went on his way.

Near Thebes, he ran into some tax collectors and cut off their ears and noses. The local ruler didn't like that and sent an army to kill Hercules. Of course, Hercules killed them instead, and the ruler, as well!

Now, for some strange reason, he became such a hero he was given a lot of prizes including a golden suit of armor, a bronze club, and a nice wife. All this attention excited Hercules so much, he lost control and killed several children who happened to be nearby. Then, Hercules went away to think up some heroic stuff, to make up for the bad things he'd done.

The Twelve Labors

To make up for the bad things he'd done, Hercules agreed to perform twelve heroic deeds. Since he was already known for killing lions, his first job was to destroy another lion whose two parents were a monster with a hundred heads, and a creature who was half-woman, half-snake.

The second task was to get rid of the Hydra, a poisonous water snake with nine heads. The Hydra's breath was so awful that anyone getting a whiff turned green and died. But Hercules held his breath and started chopping off the

nine heads, one at a time. For each head he cut off, two more grew in its place, and Hercules couldn't cut fast enough to keep up. His servant brought a burning torch, and together they destroyed the Hydra.

One of the dozen deeds he had to do was to clean out the Augean Stables, where three thousand oxen had been living for thirty years, without those stables getting so much as a good sweeping. The stables were a mess, but Hercules made a couple of rivers run through the building and washed it clean in minutes. Though Hercules didn't have to kill anything that time, that was considered a very heroic deed indeed!

The End of Hercules

One day, in a fit of madness, Hercules killed his friend Iphitus. To punish himself, he went to work as housekeeper for Queen Omphale. He gave Omphale his lion skin to wear, and he put on an apron. For three years, he washed dishes and made beds in Omphale's palace. Then he took back his lion skin and married a lady named Dejanira.

During their wedding trip, they came to a river. A centaur, which was part man and part horse, offered to give Dejanira a ride to the other bank, so she wouldn't get wet. Hercules swam across the river and waited, but the centaur didn't come. Hercules swam back and saw the creature trying to run away with his wife, so he shot it in the heart. But before the centaur died, it gave Dejanira a magic potion and said one

day she might use it to make
sure her husband still loved her.

Not long after that,
Dejanira decided Hercules was
in love with somebody else. She
soaked a robe with the magic
potion and when Hercules put
it on, the material stuck to his
flesh and killed him.

Afterward, Jupiter brought
Hercules up to Mount
Olympus and made him a god.
"Hercules is the greatest hero
of all time," decided Jupiter.
"He belongs in heaven with
me."

47

About the Author

World-famous ventriloquist and puppeteer Shari Lewis (also known as Lamb Chop's mother) has been honored with five Emmy Awards, a Peabody, the Monte Carlo TV Award for World's Best Variety Show, and the 1983 Kennedy Center Award for Excellence and Creativity in the Arts. One of the few female symphony conductors, she has performed with and conducted more than 100 symphony orchestras, including the National Symphony at the Kennedy Center, the Pittsburgh Symphony, the National Arts Centre Orchestra of Canada, and the Osaka National Symphony in Japan.

Besides the recently published *One-Minute Bible Stories—Old Testament* and *One-Minute Bible Stories—New Testament,* Shari Lewis is the author of three previous books for Doubleday—*One-Minute Bedtime Stories, One-Minute Favorite Fairy Tales* and *One-Minute Animal Stories. One-Minute Bedtime Stories* (available from Worldvision) and *One-Minute Bible Stories* (both Old and New Testament available from Magic Window/RCA/Columbia) are on home videocassettes.

Shari Lewis is presently chairman of the Board of Trustees of the International Reading Foundation and has served on the national board of the Girl Scouts of the U.S.A. A resident of Beverly Hills, California, Ms. Lewis is married to book publisher Jeremy Tarcher; their daughter, Mallory, is in the home video industry.

C. S. Ewing has been illustrating works for children that include books, textbooks, and children's magazines. She studied at the Art Institute in Kansas City, Missouri, the city where she now lives and works. She most recently illustrated *One-Minute Bible Stories—Old Testament* and *One-Minute Bible Stories—New Testament.*